HE(ART)
FORMS OF LOVE

By

Kimberly L. Bennett

Dedication

To my beautiful, smart, and kind daughter Kenya. I dedicate the "HE(ART) FORMS OF LOVE" book to you. Thank you for your help and suggestions in putting together this magnificent book. I'm the luckiest mother on earth, to have you as my daughter.

I love you!

Love, your mother
♥ Kimberly L. Bennett

Chapter 1

 My Daughter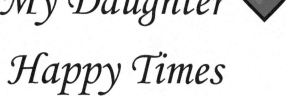

Happy Times

I Love Sugar, SC, 2021

Harold Washington Library. Chicago, IL.

Miami, Fl, Marenas Beach Resort,2018

Aunt Home, Anniversary Party, 2021

Home, 14th Birthday Party

My Room, Favorite Shirt

Me & Daughter at Knuckle Heads Play Center

Me at my Mom & Auntie Birthday party.

Kenya's at Auntie House

Chapter 2
Pictures of Foods

You put a Dent in my Heart

Protecting My Heart

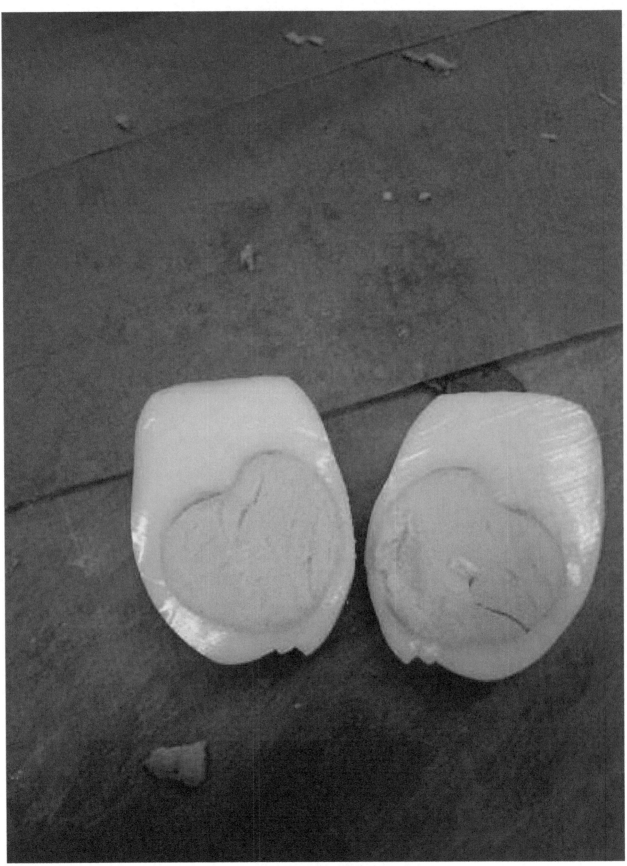

Heart-to-Heart

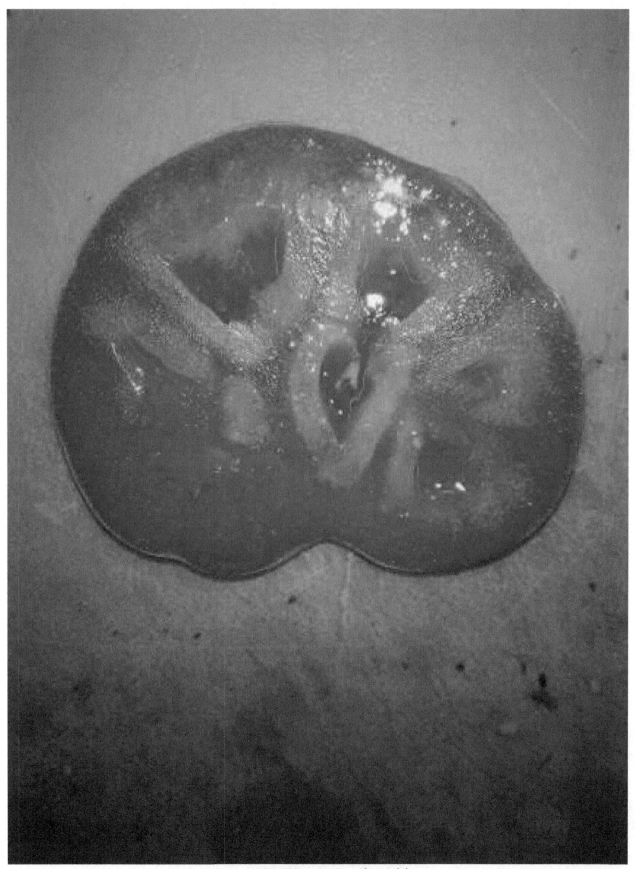

My Heart in Good Health

Queen's Breakfast

I Love Chips

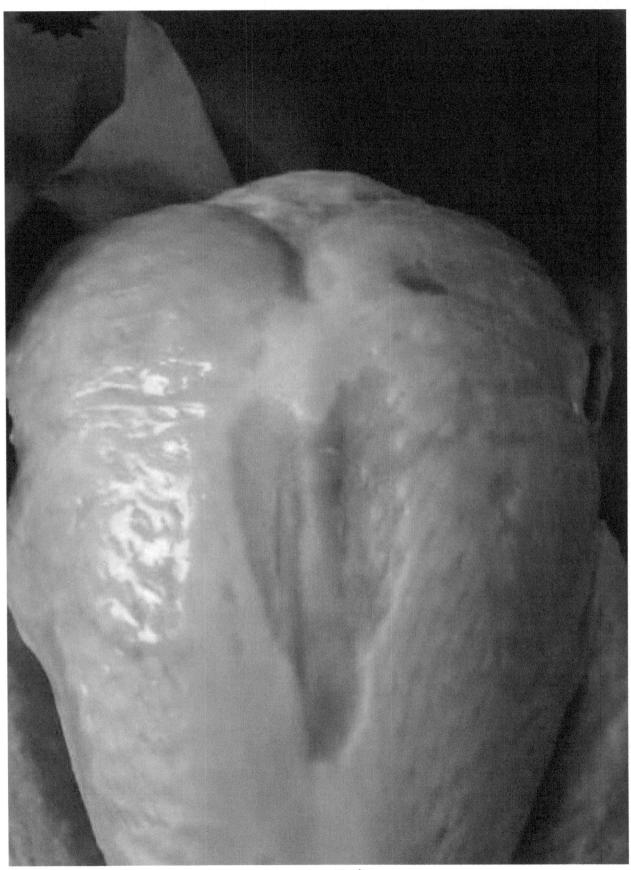

American Turkey

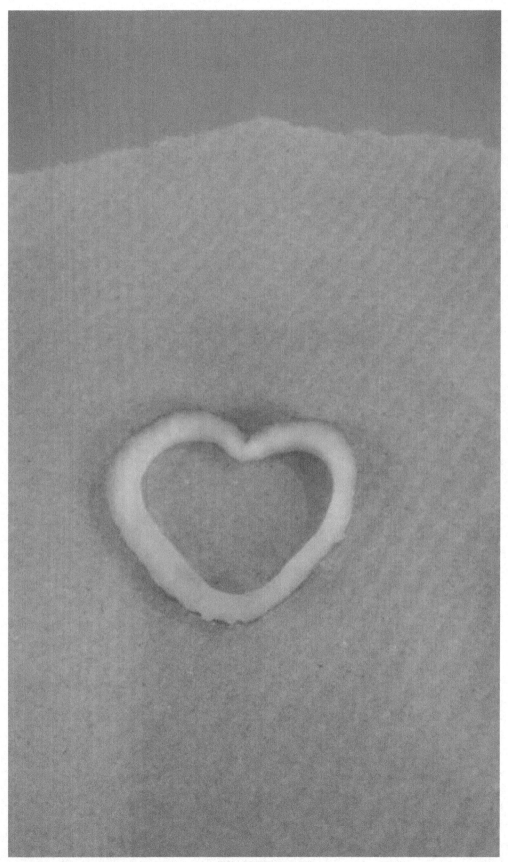

Put A Ring on It

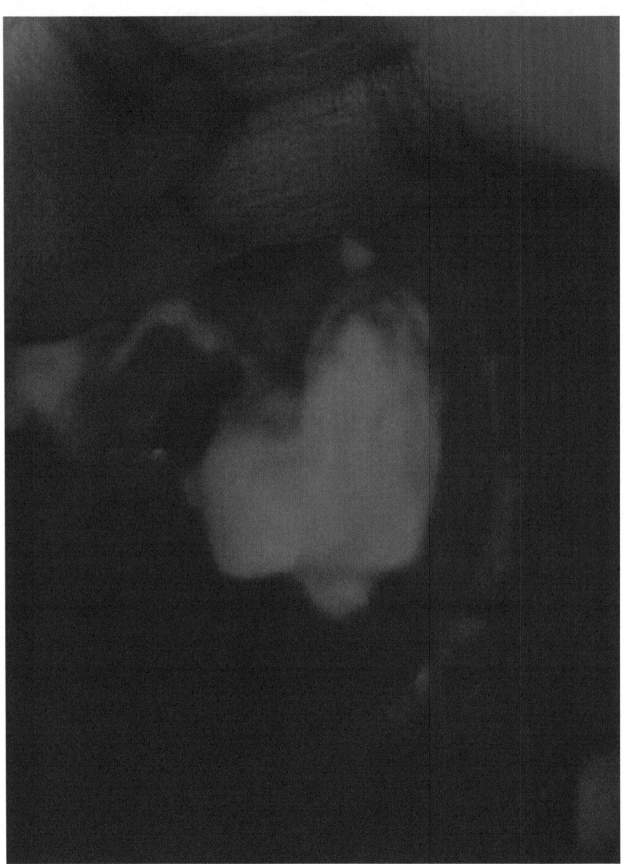

Your Love is a Drain

A Yummy Treat

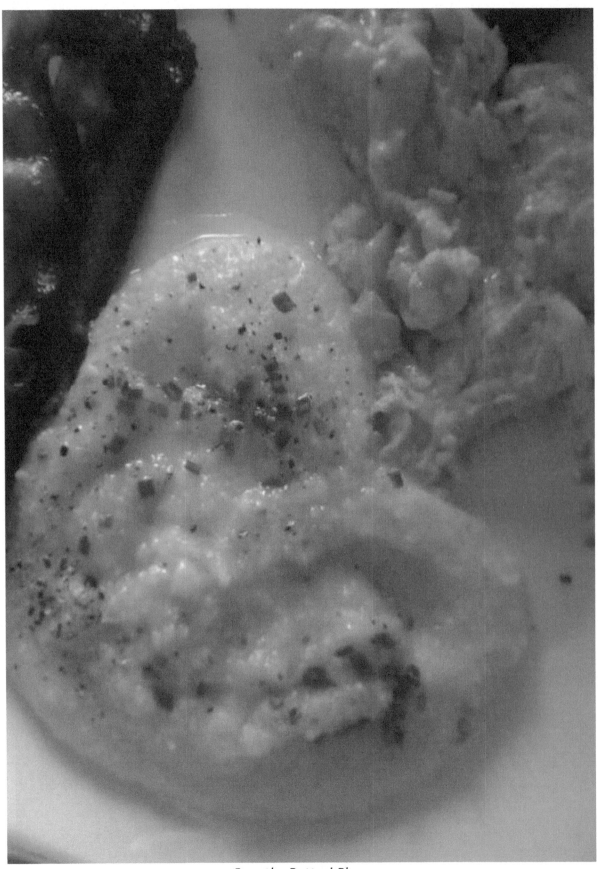

Pass the Butter! Please.

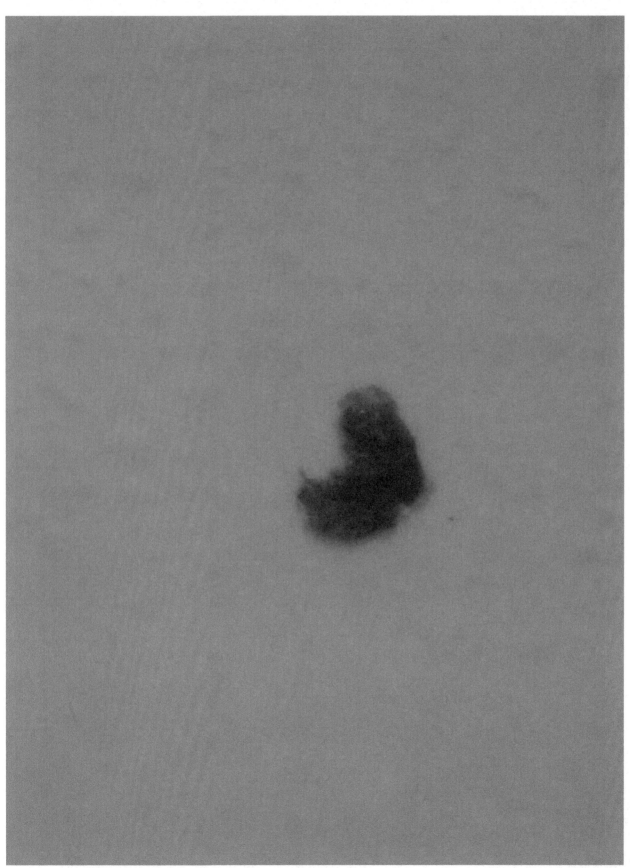

Eat your Heart out of

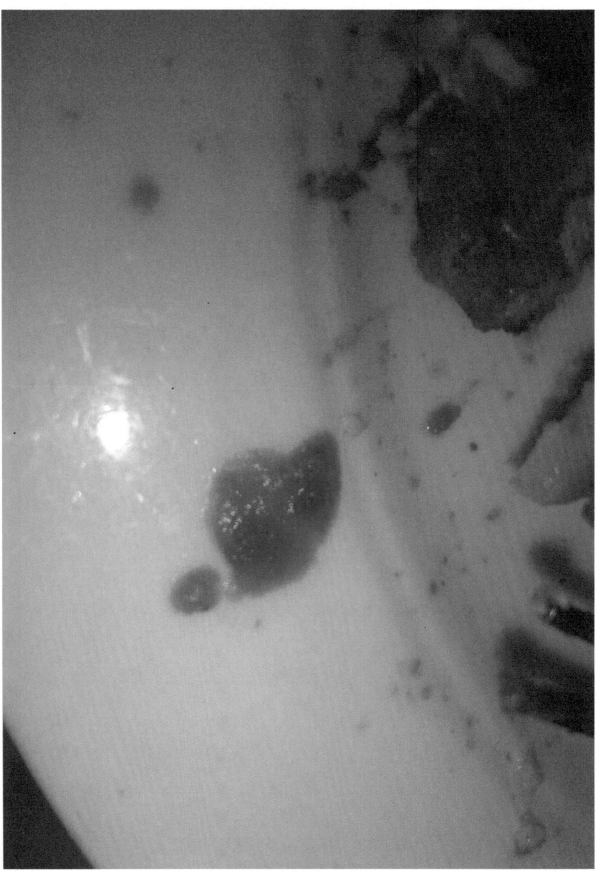

That's Amore

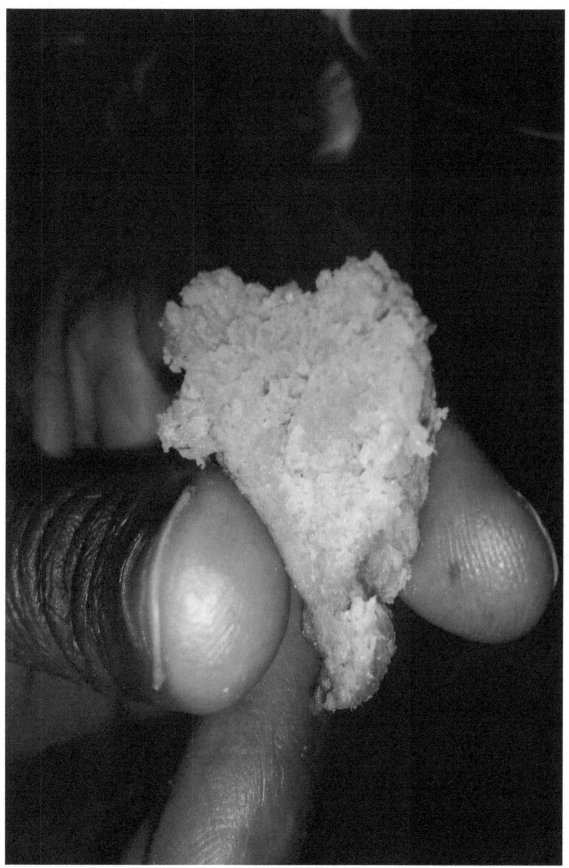

A Hearty Meat

Big Hearted

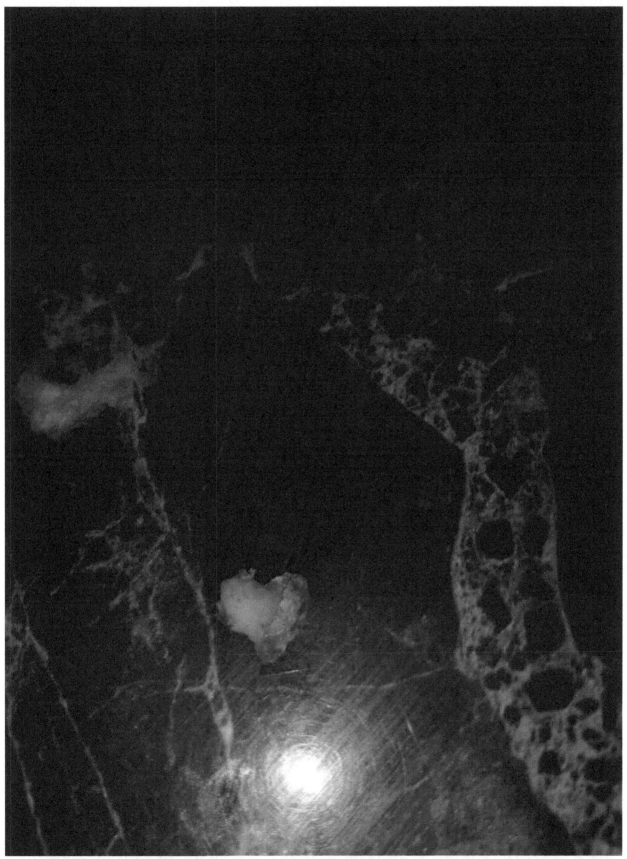

Love your Skin

The Taste is Incredible

A Sweetheart

A Love Feast

A Good Source of Fiber

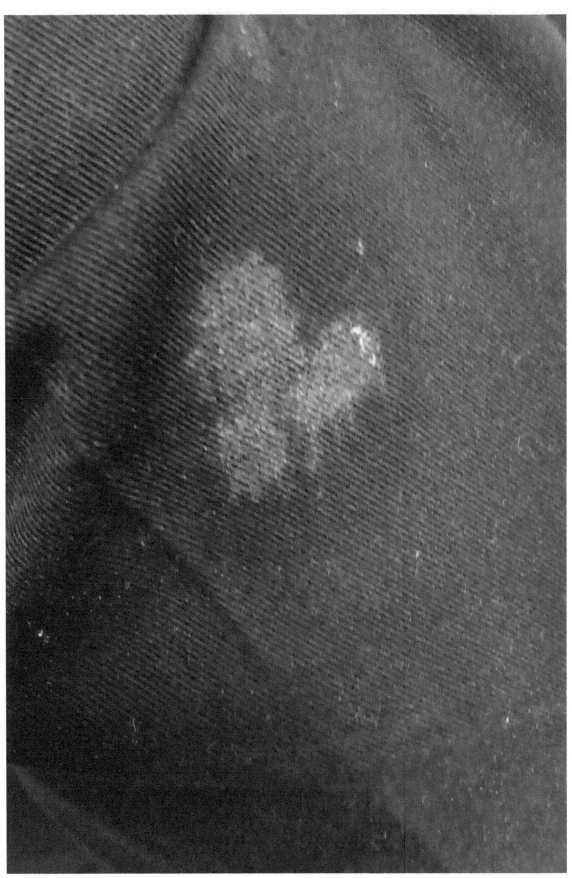

Accidentally in Love

Rippling of Love

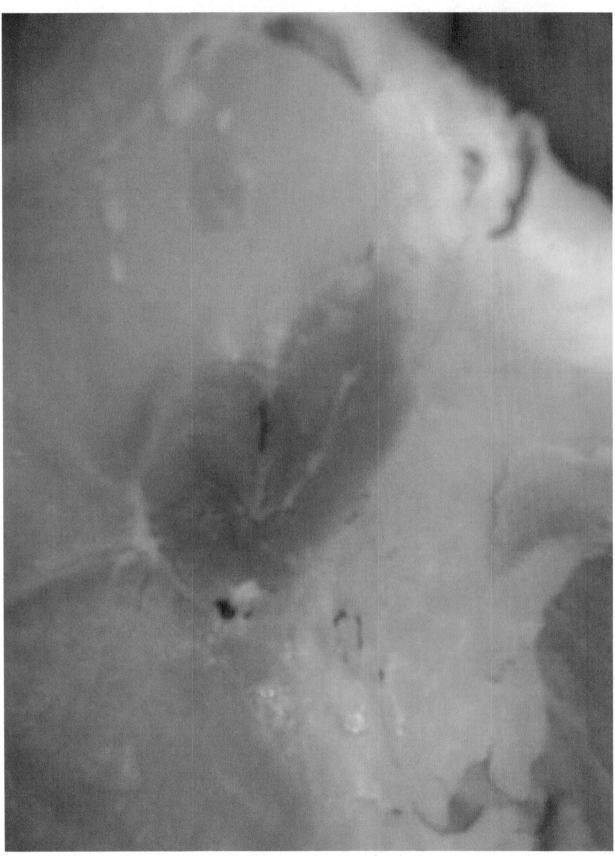

I would Love a Ham Sandwich

A Bloody Plum Heart

Source of Happiness

Chapter 3

Water Images

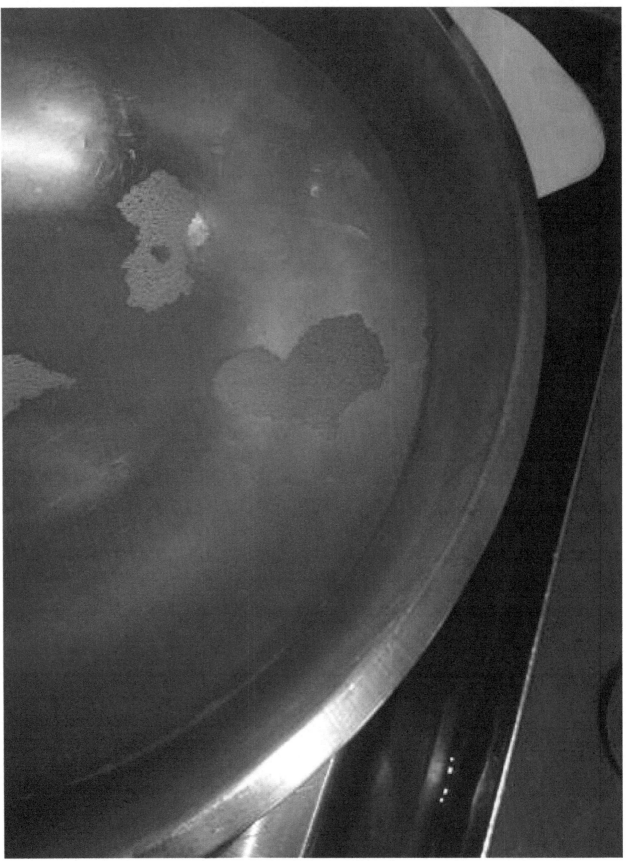

Water + Soap= Magical

Splash of Love

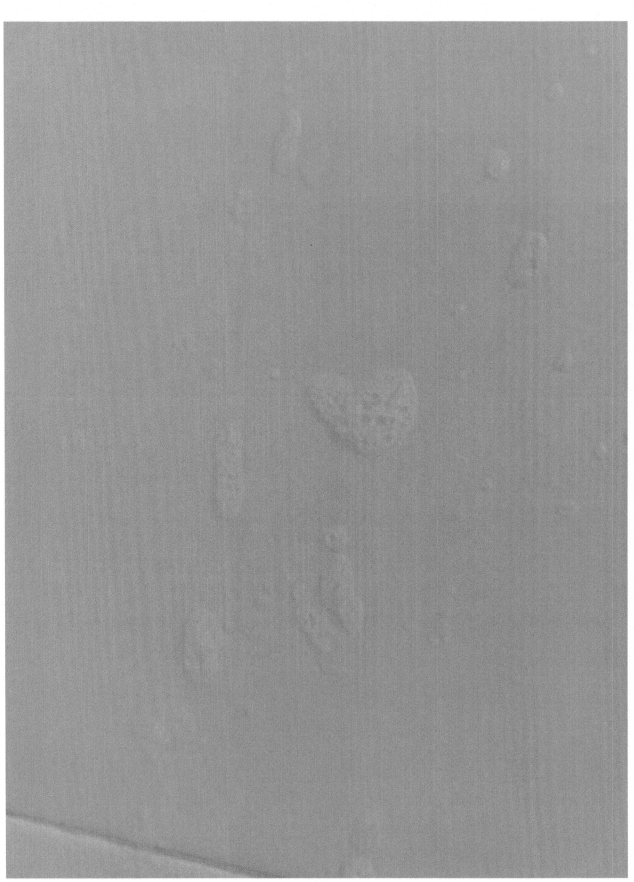

Vanishing Heart

Don't Cry over Spilled Milk

Signs of Love

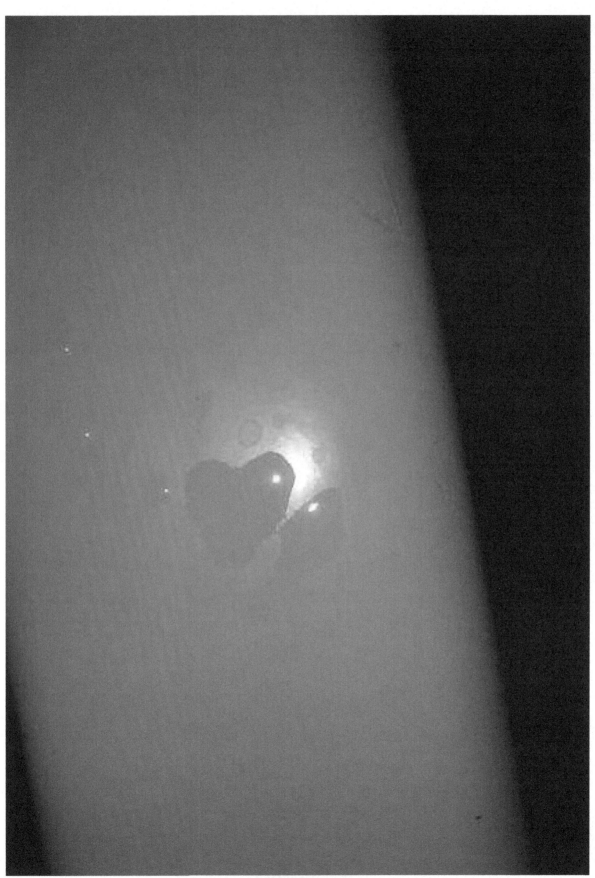

Love in All Shapes

My Sinking Heart

Home-Sweet-Home

Beauty & Love Around Us

Chapter 4

🦋 Ground Art 🐞

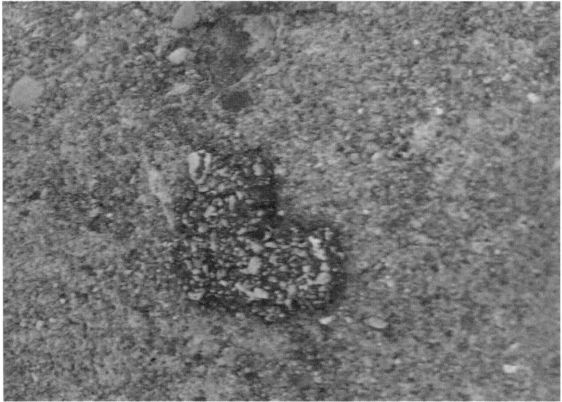

Solid Love

Stain Heart

My Dream Heart

Rainbow Heart

Washed Away Love

It's A Yellow Paper Heart

Gravel of Love

Cracked Heart

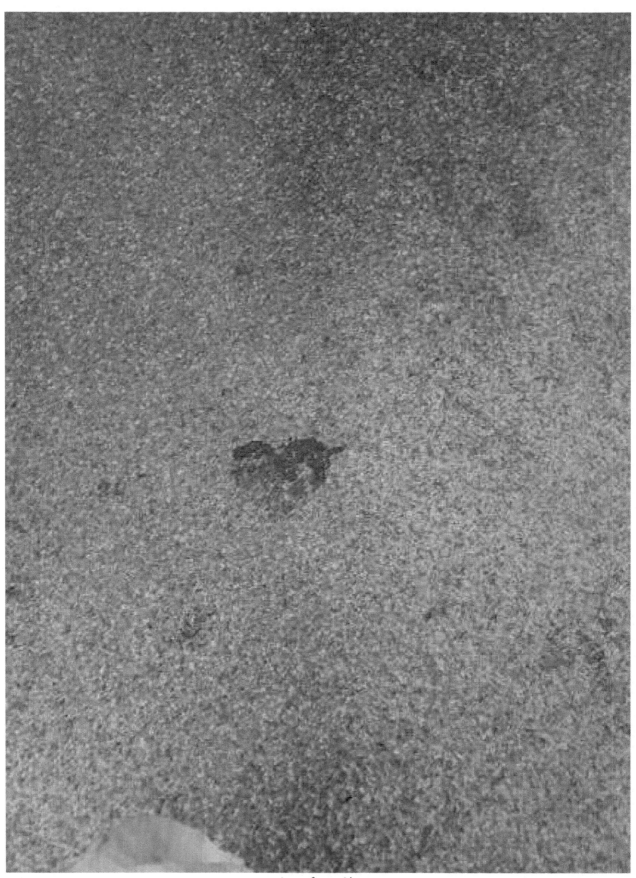

Love from Above

Purest Form of Love

Love Frozen in Time

Engraved Heart

Step-Love

Chapter 5

 Paper Shapes

In Need of Love

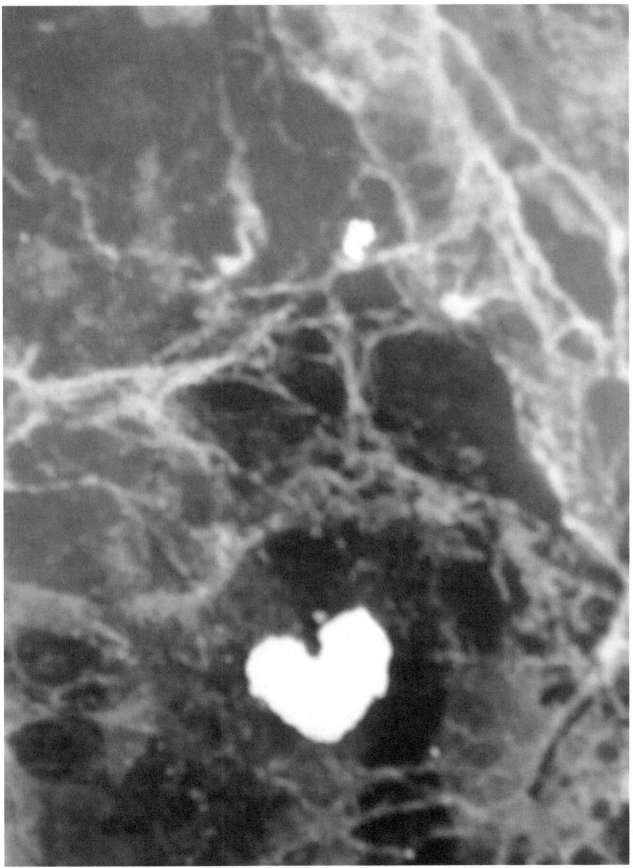

My Heart on the Table

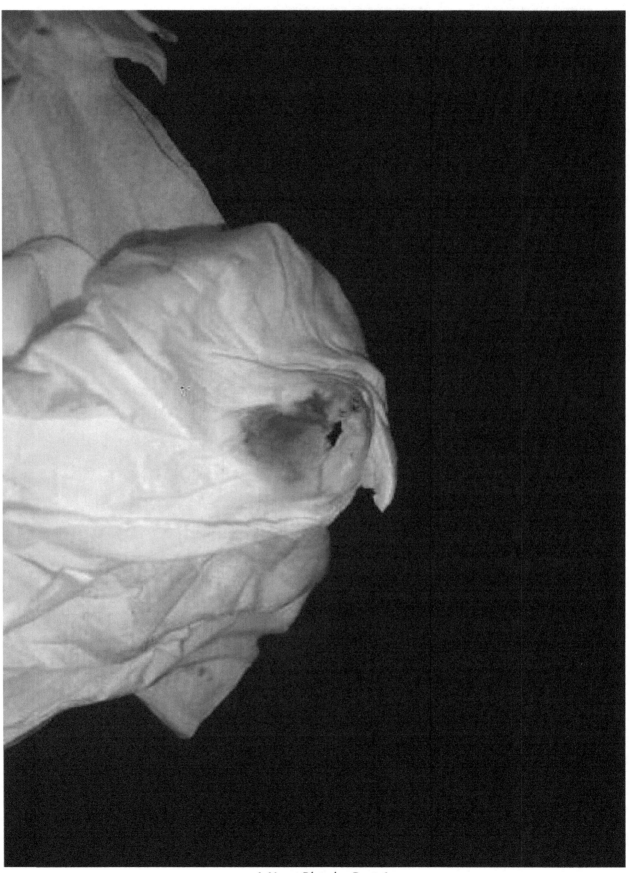

A Nose Bleed – Part 1

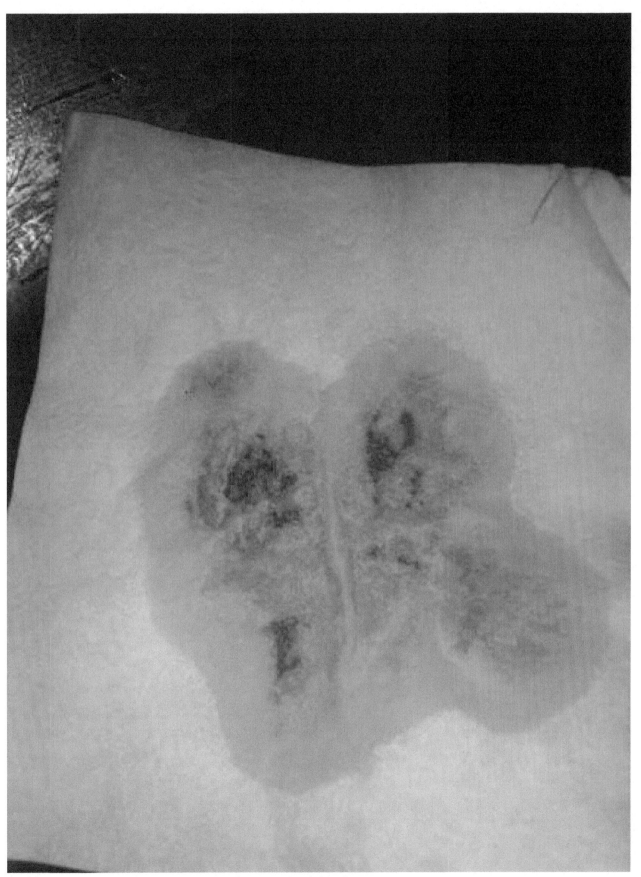

Draining Hearts

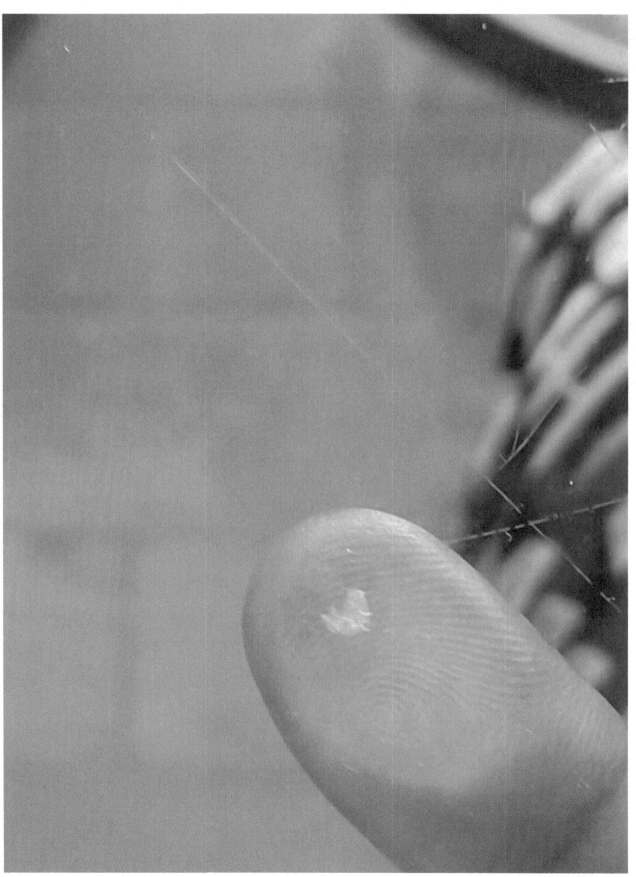

Love Yourself

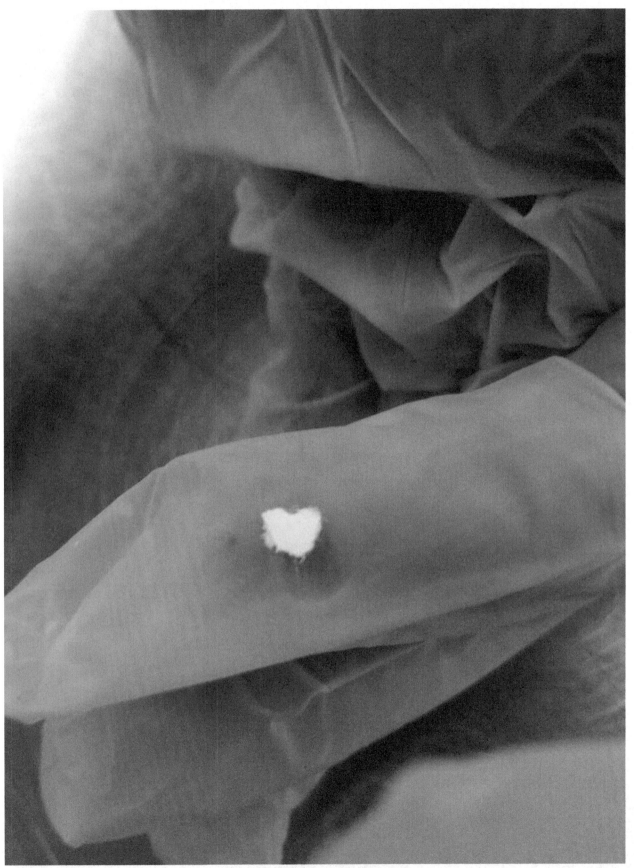

My Heart is in Your Hand

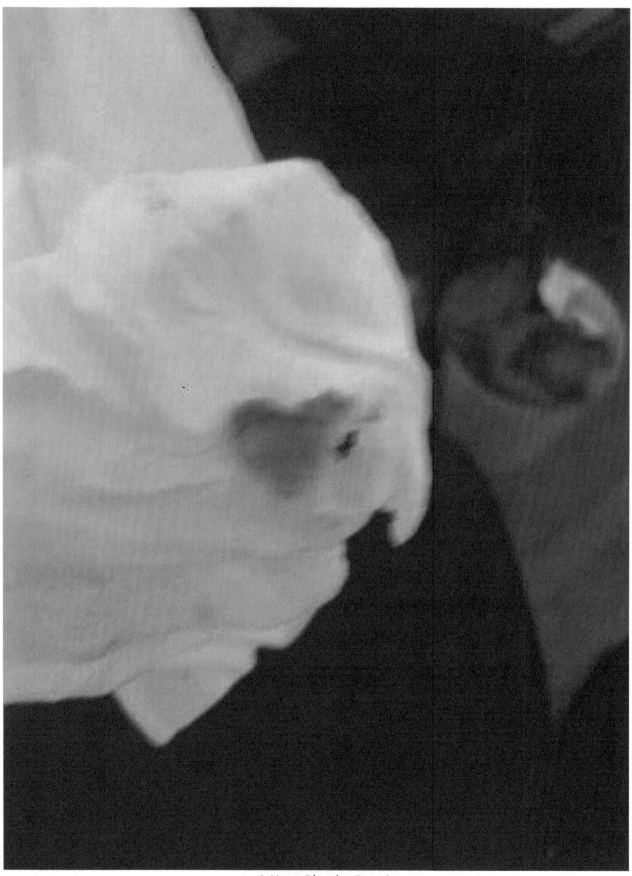

A Nose Bleed – Part 2

Chapter 6

Shadows

American Oak Stain

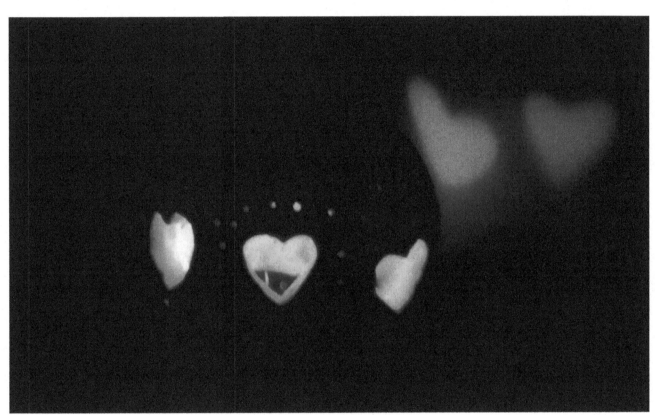

The Cinderella Story

The Shy Kid

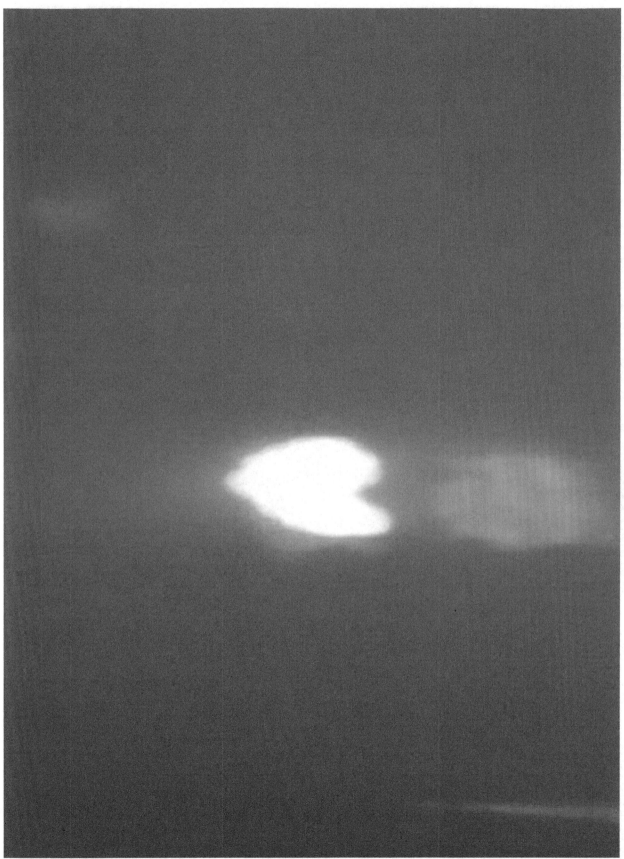

Reflection Power

A Clear Heart

Heart Seekers

Chapter 7

Bonus Pictures 📷 😍

Listen to My Heart

Mixtures of Love

The Mixtures of Love

A Love Song

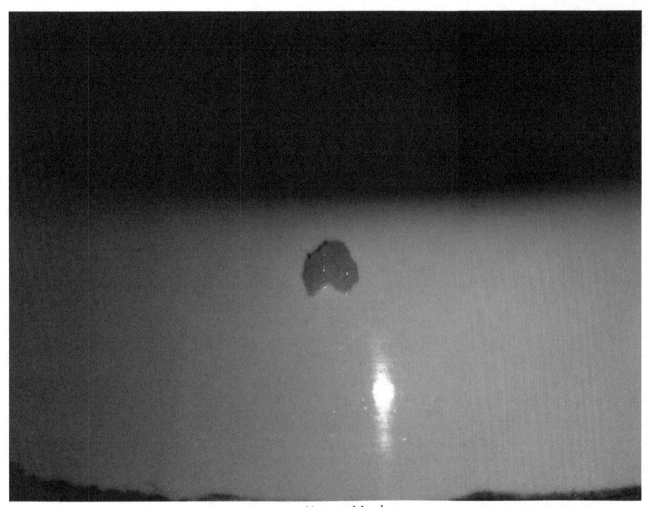

Hearty Meal

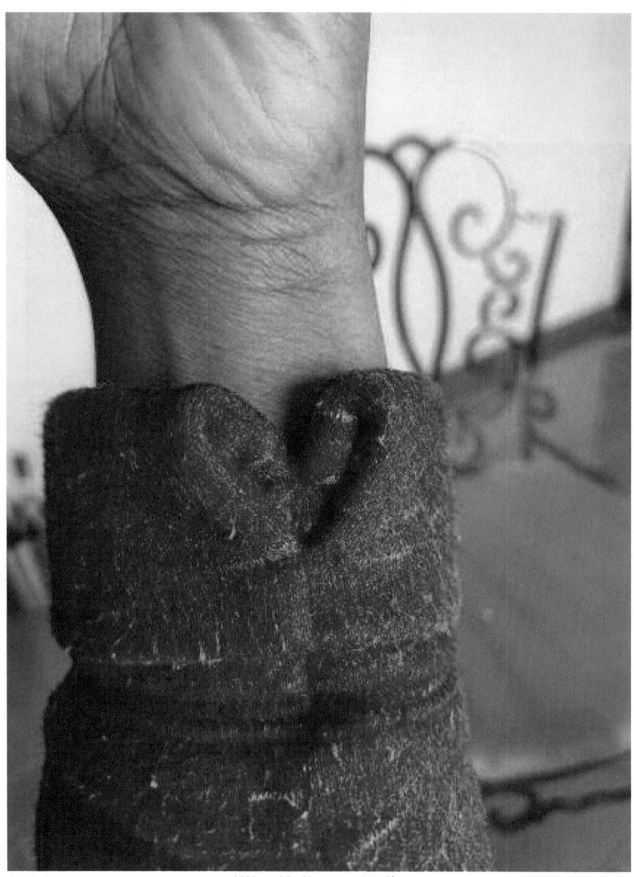

I Wear My Heart on My Sleeve

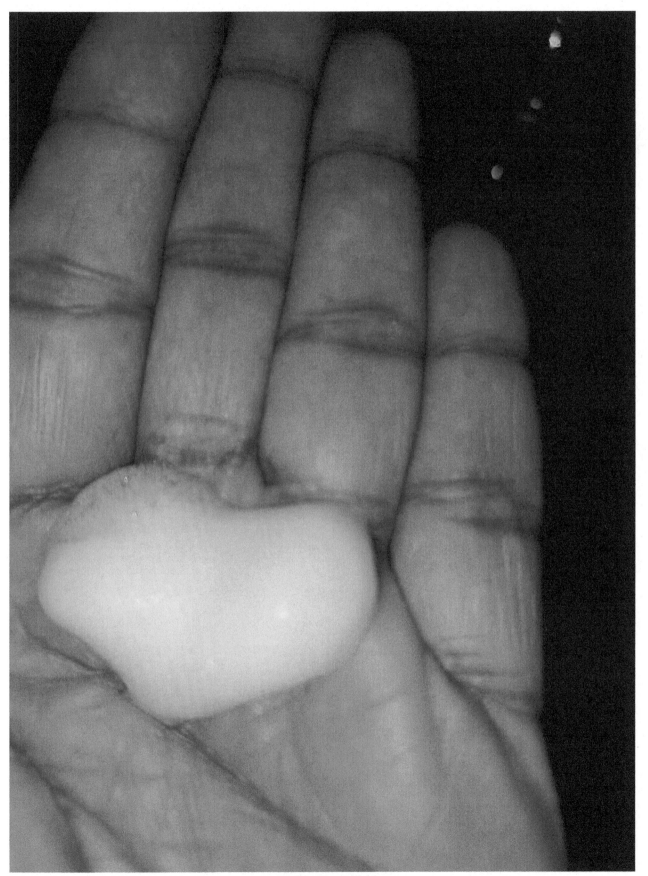

Lathering Bubbles

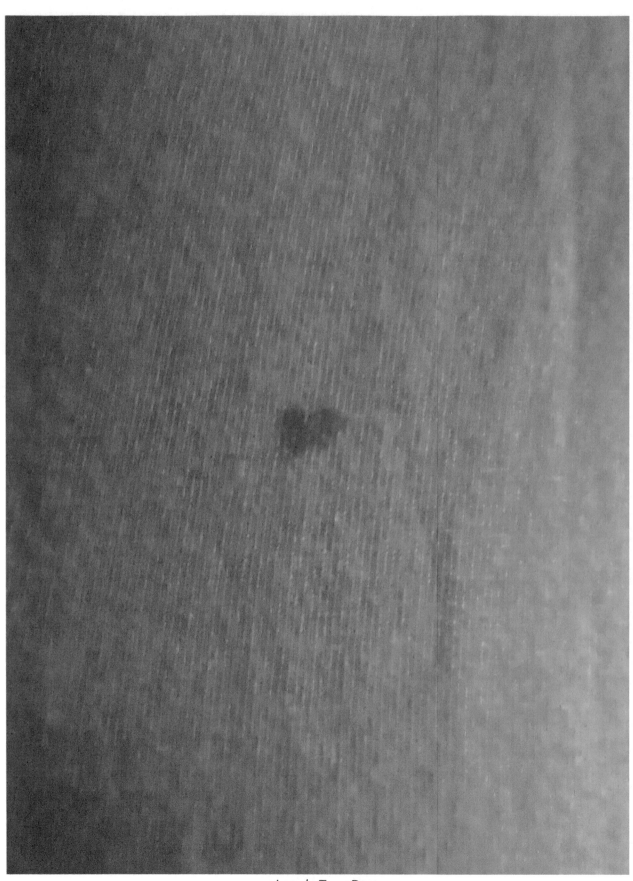

Lonely Tear Drop

crème de la creme

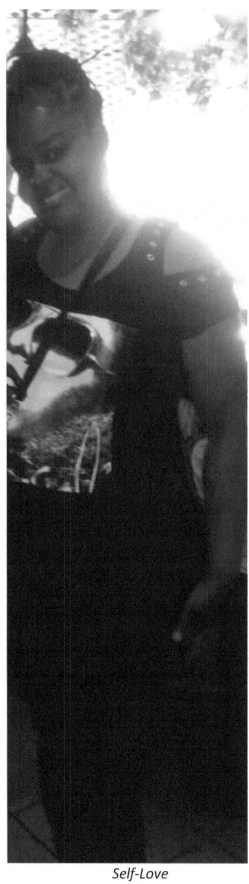

Self-Love

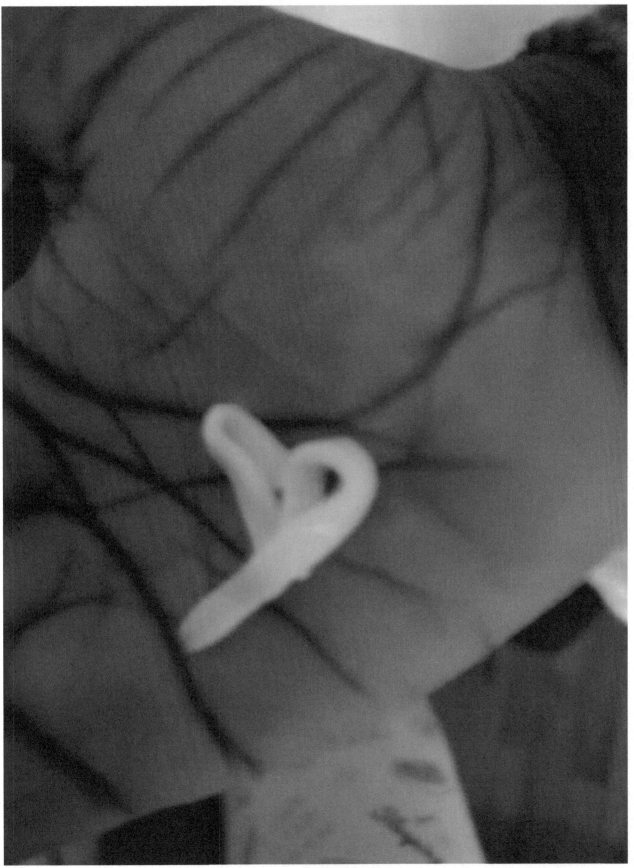

Lotion of Love

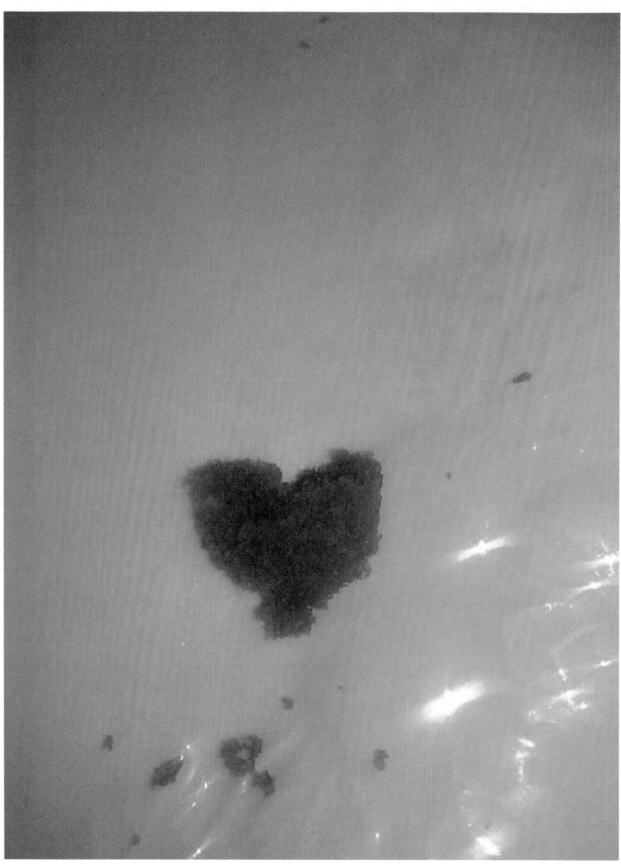

Hearty Bran

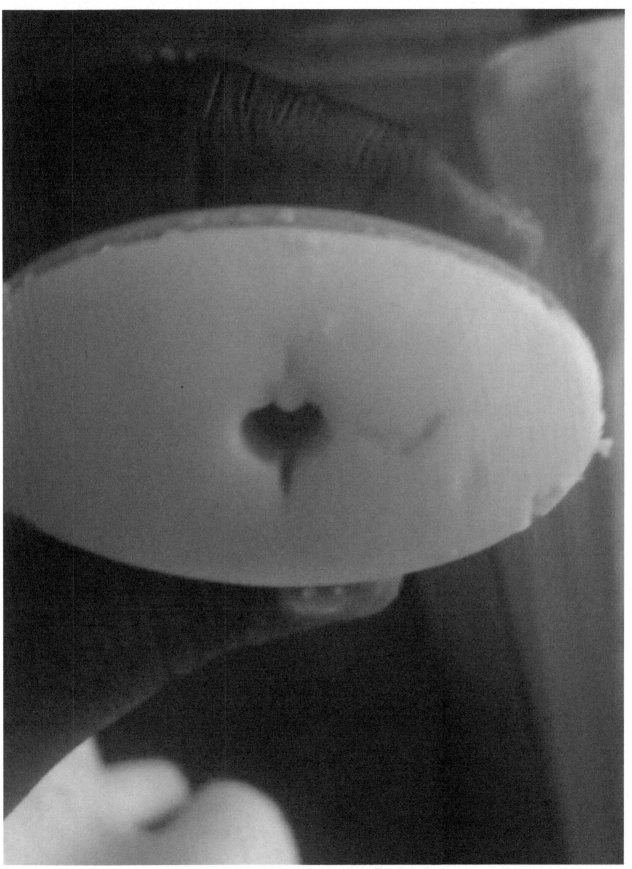

Me & My Daughter Love This Product

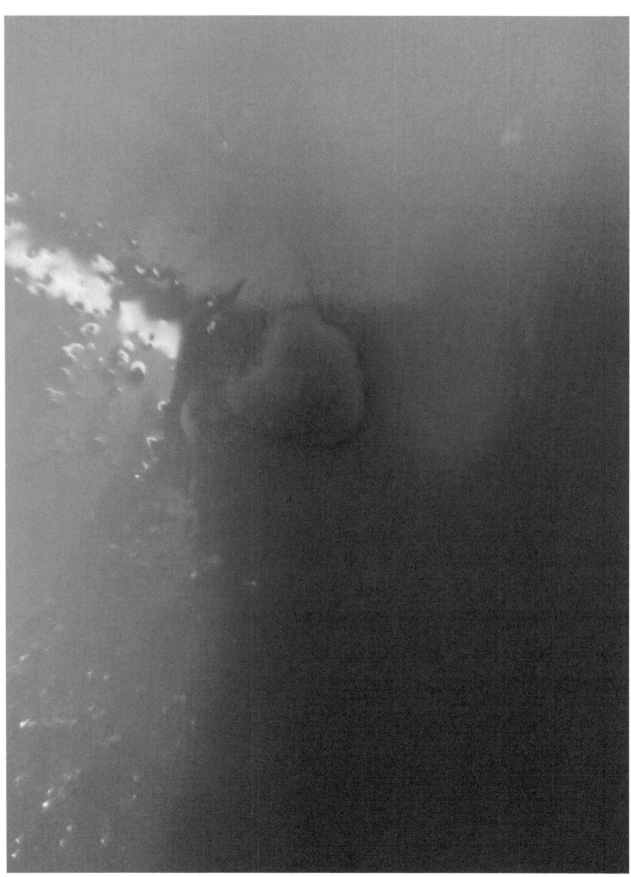

Cleaning Paste

Glam Love

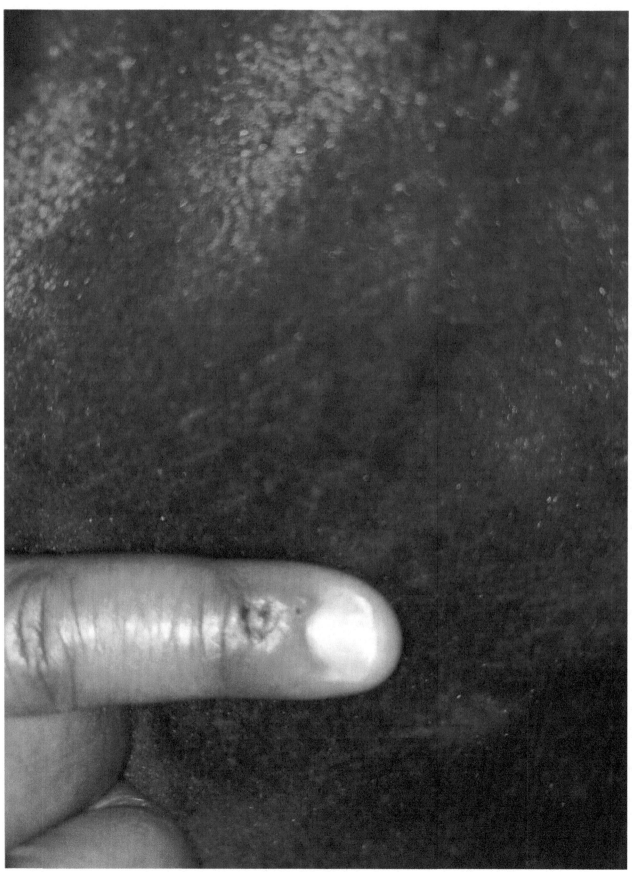

Broken-hearted

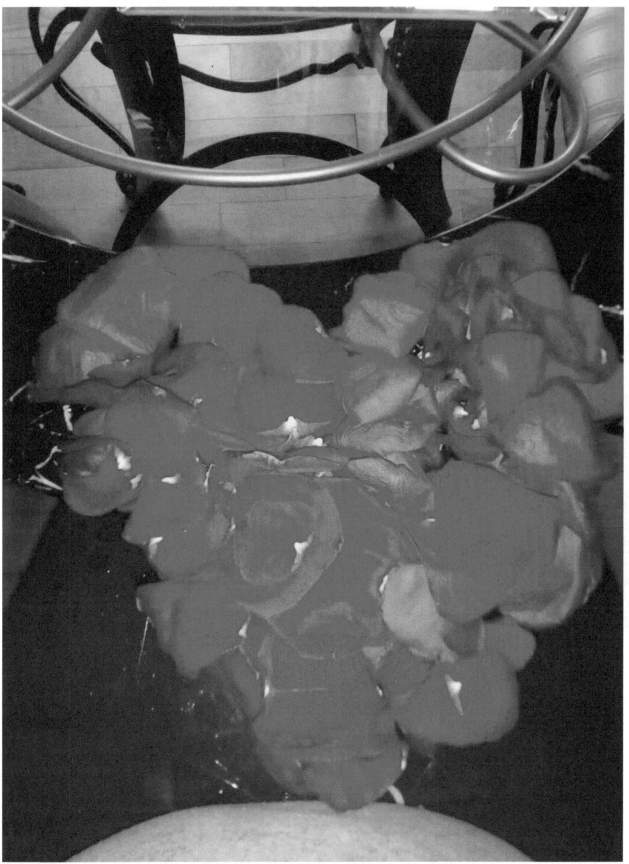

Love at First Sight

The Garden of Love

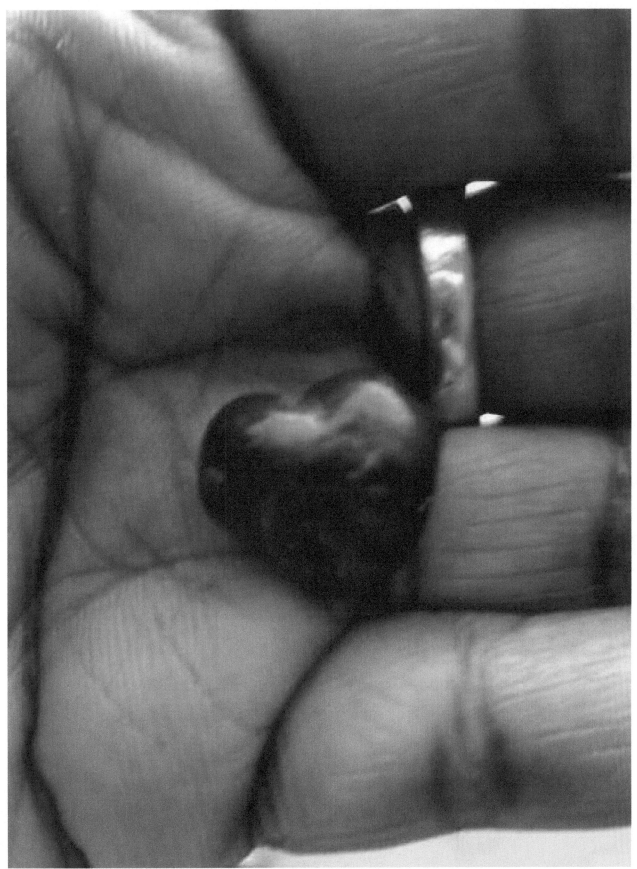

Life's Enjoyment

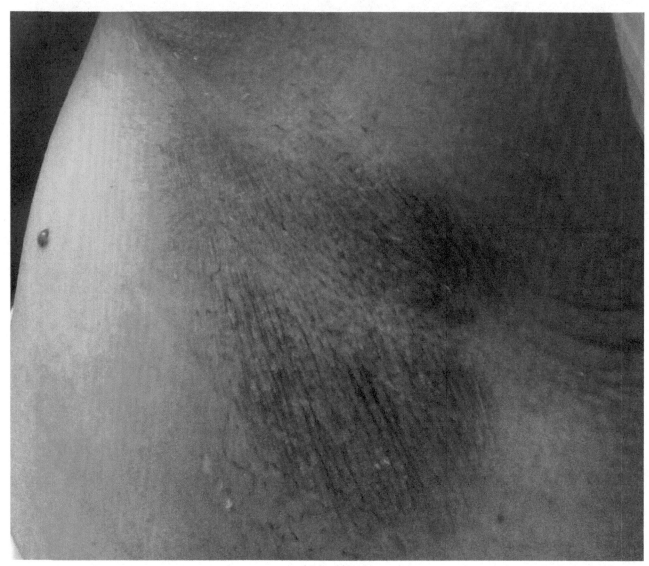

At Its Worst

Dream Hearts

You're So Appealing

A Beautiful Creation

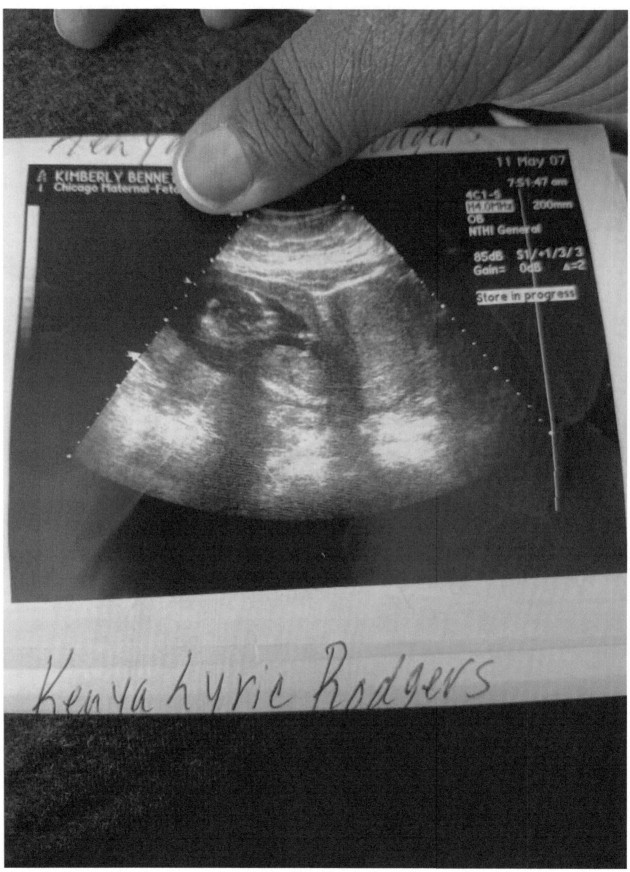

Two Hearts

The Love of Art

My Heart

Higher Love

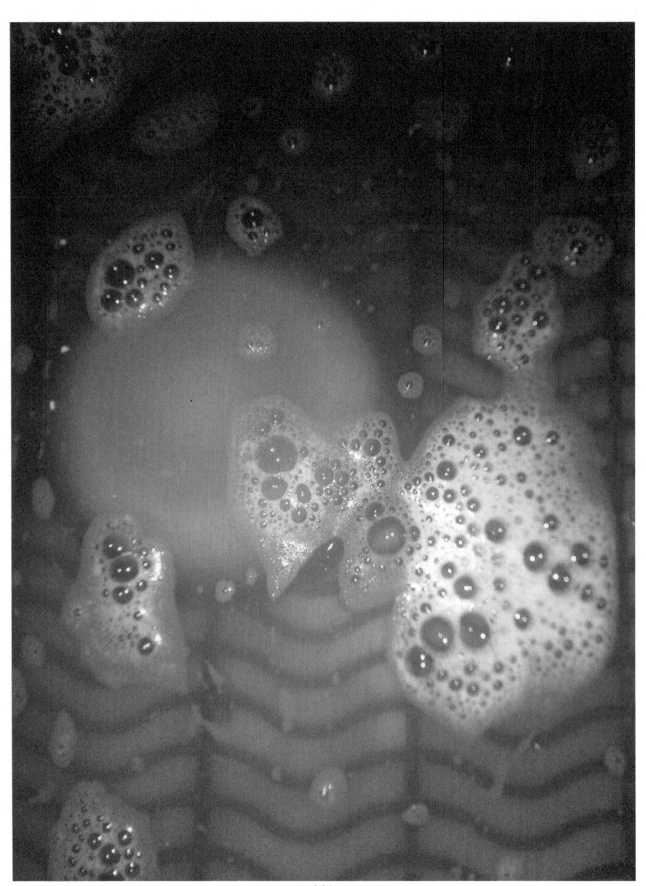

Bubbly Love

Piece of My Love

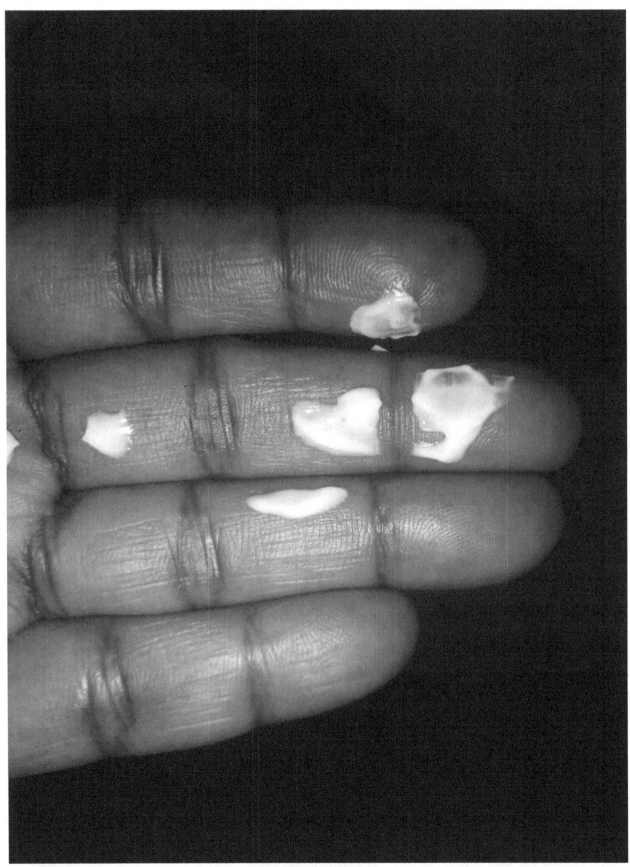

Soothing Relief

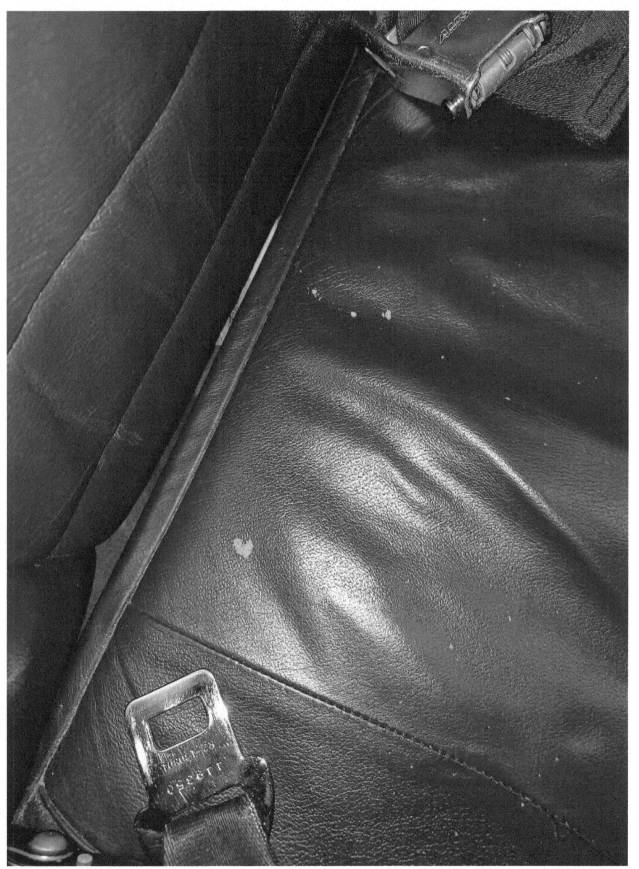

Filthy Flight Seat